The royalties of Fiep Westendorp go to the Fiep Westendorp Foundation's children's projects.
For further information: www.fiepwestendorp.nl

Jip and Janneke

Two kids from Holland

Eerste druk, 2008; tweede druk, 2009; derde druk, 2010; vierde druk, 2011; vijfde druk, 2012; zesde druk, 2013

isbn 978 90 451 0665 6 / nur 273

www.queridokinderboeken.nl

www.fiepwestendorp.nl

www.annie-mg.com

www.anniemgschmidt.nl

www.jipenjanneke.nl

Illustrations: Fiep Westendorp

Concept and editing: Gioia Smid

Texts: Gioia Smid and Hans van der Voort

Translation: Rina Vergano at Creative Translations

Design: de Brigade, Wietske Lute

Jip and Janneke
Two kids
from Holland

Fiep Westendorp

Em. Querido's Uitgeverij BV
2013

This is Jip and...

They are going to take you

...this is Janneke

on a trip through Holland.

Holland, or the Netherlands, is a small country, but lots of people live there. Jip and Janneke live next-door to each other. They look after their dog and cat together. The little birds are their friends.

Holland is ruled by a Queen.
Janneke likes to pretend that she is
Queen. Then she can give the orders!
But Jip likes to give orders too, so he
pretends that he is King!

L ots of people in Holland ride bikes. Jip and Janneke can do that too. But riding mum's bike together is tricky and dangerous! All the cats who live nearby have jumped up on the fence…

In Holland there are lots of canals, rivers and lakes. It's easy to fall in! Jip and Janneke are having swimming lessons so that they will always be safe in the water…

Holland is famous for its windmills... and its fields full of tulips. Jip picks a beautiful bunch of tulips, all different colours, for Janneke. And the birds have a little present for Janneke too!

Jip and Janneke can see which day or month it is by looking at the calendar. There are four seasons in the year: spring, summer, autumn and winter. Jip and Janneke are going to show you what they do in Holland all through the year.

Spring

Holland has many beaches. But in springtime the sea is too cold to swim in. It's even too cold for paddling in. Brave Jip and Janneke do it anyway! But they do keep their shoes on...

At Easter, Dutch children paint
eggs. It's a lot of fun.
Jip and Janneke can make as much mess
as they like because they are wearing
aprons!

In Holland the grown-ups hide Easter
eggs in the garden and the children have
to find them. Jip and Janneke are looking for the hidden eggs. The dog and the
cat are looking too...

J ip gives Janneke a beautiful Easter bunny. Janneke and the cat have never seen such a lovely one before. It's made of chocolate, but how can you eat such a beautiful animal...?

Summer

In Holland the sun shines in the summer and it's lovely and warm. Sometimes it's so hot that Jip and Janneke don't feel like playing. Even the cat is too lazy to chase the birds...

S ometimes Jip and Janneke go to the city farm. There are lots of hens and cockerels and ducks. Sometimes the hens lay their eggs in the grass. And the peacock likes to show off his beautiful tail…

When the weather is fine, Jip and Janneke have a picnic in the country-side. When the cow comes to have a look, Janneke is so frightened that she runs away. Aha, thinks the dog, now I can steal her biscuit!

W hen it's hot, the ice-cream man comes round. If Jip and Janneke have been good, then they can have an ice-cream. The cat and the birds have been good too, but they don't get anything...

Autumn

In the autumn it can be very windy in Holland. Then Jip and Janneke fly their kites. But watch out for the branches of the trees, they will grab a kite if they can!

In the autumn it rains a lot in Holland. But Jip and Janneke just put on their raincoats and their rubber boots. Then they can stamp about in the puddles without getting wet...

When the weather turns cold, most birds fly away to the warm South. Jip and Janneke feed their little feathered friends who have stayed behind, so at least they won't be hungry.

The funfair has come to town! Jip and Janneke like the merry-go-round best of all. The man rings the bell and the children whizz round and round.
It makes them a little bit dizzy...

Winter

Sometimes it is very cold in wintertime. Then Jip and Janneke wear woolly hats and gloves. It's so cold that even the dog, the cat and the little bird might need woolly socks...

J ip and Janneke see St. Nicholas on
the street outside the school.
All the children are happy because
St. Nicholas has come to visit. Maybe
they could sneak inside with the other
children...?

On the fifth of December it is the feast of St. Nicholas.

St. Nicholas rides over the rooftops at night on his horse and throws presents down the chimneys. Dutch children put their shoes by the fireplace and sing songs for St. Nicholas. Jip and Janneke sing beautifully. They are hoping that St. Nicholas might leave them a present or two in their shoe!

Sometimes it freezes so hard in Holland that a thick layer of ice covers the canals and ditches. Then everyone goes skating. Jip and Janneke can't skate very well yet. But they can skate better than the dog and the cat.
They can only slide a bit...

When it's nearly Christmas, Jip
and Janneke are allowed to decorate
the Chrismas tree. They hang up lots of
glass balls and paperchains. And little
silver birds too. Some glass balls fall on
the floor, but luckily they don't break!

J ip and Janneke have made a snowman. He has a carrot for a nose, but he doesn't have any legs. So the children put him on the sledge and take him out for a walk.

Jip and Janneke have told you all sorts of things about their lives in Holland. If you ever come to Holland, maybe you will bump into Jip and Janneke. Then you can tell them all about life in your country. Goodbye Jip, goodbye Janneke, see you again soon!

The history of Jip and Janneke

Jip and Janneke (pronounced Yip and Yannaka) are the Netherlands' most famous tots. From 1952 right up to today, generations of Dutch children have grown up with them. Parents read these stories to their children, just as they were read them by their own parents when they were young.

The adventures of Jip and Janneke were published weekly between 1952 and 1957 on the children's page of the Dutch newspaper *Het Parool* (The Watchword). Leading Dutch children's author Annie M. G. Schmidt wrote the stories and Fiep Westendorp illustrated them. Fiep Westendorp chose to depict the children as silhouettes. These characteristic black-and-white illustrations were clearly recognisible and could be easily reproduced in newsprint. Because of their enormous popularity, the adventures were published each year from 1953 in book form too.

From 1976 Fiep Westendorp produced weekly colour illustrations to accompany the old stories for the under-fives' comic *Bobo*. In that happy world of colour the figures of Jip and Janneke remained as black-and-white silhouettes, although Fiep Westendorp changed their outward appearance radically: Jip and Janneke turned from lanky-limbed children of around seven years of age into young tots with compact bodies and an almost caricatural quality. It took Fiep Westendorp until 1984 to replace all the illustrations.

Whilst Annie M. G. Schmidt often introduced an adult into the stories, Fiep Westendorp chose to depict Jip and Janneke without their parents or other adults. In this way, Fiep believed, children would be better able to identify with the figures she drew. She would only draw an adult if she absolutely had to: for instance, an ice-cream man or a swimming instructor.

Even today, after more than fifty years, all Dutch under-fives love Jip and Janneke. They carry or wear their black-and-white silhouettes on their school bags, lunchboxes, swimming costumes, towels, pyjamas, raincoats, and so on. For almost twenty years, Jip and Janneke have been a leading brand for the Dutch chainstore HEMA. And to date, Jip and Janneke books have sold more than five million copies. Regardless of their ethnic background, Dutch children identify strongly with Jip and Janneke. The fact that all children can recognise themselves in the silhouettes of Jip and Janneke, regardless of the colour of their skin, was of paramount importance to Fiep Westendorp, who died in 2004.

In this book full of colour plates, Fiep Westendorp's illustrations are the starting point of a journey through the Netherlands in which Jip and Janneke show children from other countries a number of typical events in the lives of Dutch children.